How To Be Asian

ISBN-13: 978-0-646-58920-6

How To be Asian Website

www.howtobeasianbook.com
Email: contact@howtobeasianbook.com
Facebook: www.facebook.com/howtobeasian

HOW TO BE ASIAN

FOREWORD

Stereotypes are everywhere; they have permeated various societies worldwide. They can be applied to different types of people, such as the common stereotypes that police officers like donuts and coffee, blondes are dumb, teachers love apples, or that smart people are boring. However, most stereotypes are found in specific races, ethnicities, or countries. It is the general belief that African-Americans are good at any sport, Hispanics are masters of everything car-related, Hawaiians are hula dancers, Germans and Irishmen are drunks, and that the French are always rude.

Many people from the above countries or ethnicities likely fall into these stereotypes but that hardly means the above are true for every person that belongs to any one of those groups. As such, this book is not meant to be taken seriously; it is merely a humorous and satirical glimpse into what it can be like for Asian people to live with the stereotypes attached to their race.

At this point, you have picked up this book and you might be thinking, "Why would anyone want to focus on Asian stereotypes?" It would be a hilarious read. Most of the generalizations aimed at Asians are ridiculously funny; in fact, Asian people will actually use what is in this book to stereotype themselves and be proud of it, which is actually a stereotype in itself. Hurts your brain, doesn't it? Fear not, for the purpose of this book is to shed some light on the various aspects of Asian culture that are considered "quintessentially Asian."

This book will focus on one specific stereotype at a time. The average person will likely not be familiar with most of the Asian stereotypes beyond the ones about them being good at math or not being able to drive a car to save their lives. By focusing on one stereotype at a time, the reader will grow to appreciate each one for what it is. Chuckling at an Asian friend who takes off their shoes at your front door will be more fulfilling if you understand the reasons why they're doing it. Ignorant mirth just isn't as much fun.

Following the descriptions of each stereotype will be a short list. For those of you reading this book that happen to be Asian, these lists will serve as a guide on how to be "more Asian" if you grew up in a less traditional household or outside of your mother country. For the other folks reading this book, these lists will be an invaluable source of (exaggerated) information on how to spot Asian stereotypes as you observe the world and the people in it.

After you've finished reading this book, you will either have a newfound appreciation for the quirks of your own Asian culture or you will be able to understand just a little bit more why Asian people are the way they are. So sit back, relax on the couch or in your favorite squashy chair, and enjoy this fun-filled journey into the aspects of the Far Eastern culture that are sure to tickle your funny bone.

Let's get started...

ANIME

Originally created in Japan, Anime is based on a vivid, complex and dense drawing style unique to a particular culture. "Anime" is an abbreviation for the Japanese form of the English word "animation".

The main difference between anime and traditional cartoons is the style of art. In the past, anime was referred to as "Japanimation". The style of anime art itself is instantly recognizable with distinct, sharply-realized, detailed action. More traditional character features include wild or bizarre hair styles, exaggeratedly large expressive eyes, overly-large body parts, and familiar emoji (picture characters or emoticons used in Japanese electronic messages and webpages).

The subject matter of Anime is wide ranging and can include almost any genre such as love, adventure, science fiction and anything in between. Artistic license is taken by many anime creators, including over exaggeration of limbs and height, overuse of exclamatory phrases and melodramatic facial expressions.

Many characters even produce a "massive sweat-drop" if they're embarrassed or stressed, and a red blush or set of parallel lines beneath the eyes when trying to hide romantic feelings.

Branching out into books, action figures, toys, television and feature length movies, anime is a marketing phenomenon already worth over $4.35 billion in the United States alone. Because of its far-reaching effects, anime is receiving worldwide attention and devotion, and continues to be globally popular among its very passionate fans everywhere. Thanks to the rise of the internet, anime went from being a regionally-influenced art form mostly in Asia, and found its way into the global community. Thanks to a huge fan following, anime has even led to more acceptance of Japanese culture in general.

HOW TO BECOME A HUGE ANIME FAN

1. Style your hair into the wildest, weirdest, spikiest anime hairdo you can manage, on a daily basis. This requires a lot of hair gel and brightly colored hair dye.

2. Go online and research all the newest anime you can find. Join fan sites and chat about characters like they're your best friends.

3. Stay closeted up in your room for most of your life, watching anime re-runs.

4. Stand in front of the mirror and copy the over-exaggerated facial expressions of anime characters. Whenever you smile, your eyes close.

5. Dress up as your favourite character to your nearest convention. Use your costume to preserve your virginity for the next 1000 years.

ASIANS ALL LOOK THE SAME

"Asians all look the same." "Are you guys related?"

These are common remarks that white people ask us Asians, but that's alright. Sometimes I can't tell my white friends apart either. Living in Adelaide, I find myself myself totally confused by the endless Australian accents and Xerox-copied faces swarming around me.

Everyone has watched a comedy movie or TV show and heard the phrase, "All black people look alike." Although it's not usually mentioned in shows or movies, the same thing can be said about Asian people. It takes a practiced eye to tell a Vietnamese person and a Korean person apart. You can bet that a Chinese girl will get mistaken for Filipino or Japanese. In fact, she'll probably get mistaken for any Asian ethnicity except her own. Maybe it's because of the eye-slant thing, or the cheekbones. It could be that we have similar Asian foods, designer clothes (for a bargain!) or souped-up "Fast and Furious" looking cars. Or maybe it's just because non-Asians are a little too clueless to figure out the tell-tale physical differences between a round-faced Chinese person and an oval-faced Japanese kid.

In reality, it's probably because they're too quick to believe what Hollywood tells them about Asians: we're all Jackie Chan or Jet Li, and it doesn't really matter where we're from because they're never going to visit there, anyway.

On an unrelated note, China did really well in the London Olympics, didn't they? Like, how did just one person win all those medals? It's insane.

HOW TO LOOK LIKE A TYPICAL ASIAN PERSON

1. Get a typical Asian hairstyle. Refer to pictures of Jackie Chan or any of the popular mangas for hints.

2. Avoid all forms of sunlight, and UV rays. Asians pride themselves on the ability to maintain ivory-colored skin, while non-Asians are running to the tanning salons. Crazy white people!

3. Over-emphasize the slant or squint of your eyes. Use eyeliner and mascara to help out where nature let you down. You want them so that you can be easily blinded by fishing line.

4. People on the street will come up to you and say "You look familiar." Tell them you're actually Jackie Chan. Use your new followers for world domination.

ASIAN PARENTS

Asian parents; the source of every Asian child's depression, fear, and irritation.

One of the most difficult things about growing up in an Asian household is putting up with Asian parents. Asian parents are the people who gave birth to you; therefore, they feel they can control everything about you – your appearance, your personality, and what you do in your spare time.

Speaking of spare time, it's pretty much non-existent with an Asian parent. Anything that isn't studying is a waste of time to them. They are harsh in their criticism, high in their expectations, and claim their brutal honesty only comes with good intentions.

If you're an Asian child, you will be expected to grow up and become an astrophysicist, a doctor that finds the cure for cancer, a Nobel Prize winner, or all of the above. You'll also be told that you are not living up to your potential if you get a B in chemistry.

They can get abusive if you fail to meet their expectations. Got a B on your report card? Get smacked by a wooden spoon. Stay up until 2 a.m. playing video games? Get a shoe thrown at you and your computer taken away. Didn't get into a superior college like Harvard or Oxford? If they own a set of samurai swords, you should start running now.

If you are a girl and you happen to have a brother, you can bet that there will be double-standards to deal with while growing up. Your brother will be allowed to date when he's 14 but you can't date until you're 30. His curfew is 11pm, yours is noon. He can go out of town with his friends to go camping, but you need be escorted to the mall. It will happen.

HOW TO MAKE YOUR ASIAN PARENTS GO INSANE

1. When your parents pressure you about going to Harvard or Yale, inform them you have decided to skip formal education.

2. Drop the F-Bomb while having dinner with your family. Your father will ask why you didn't drop the A-Bomb instead.

3. Decide you don't want to become a doctor. Your mother will wish she aborted you.

4. Fail your pregnancy test. This will conflict your parents.

5. Tell your Asian parents you're marrying a black man. This will work especially well if you are male.

ASIAN POP MUSIC

A music world of its own, Asian Pop comes in many diverse styles. In Japan it's called J-Pop and the wildly-popular boy/girl band music from Korea is K-Pop. And let's not forget China's contribution, called, you guessed it, C-Pop.

Over time, the Western world transformed its pop music. Although Asian pop music saw a similar change, even today it's still largely dominated by the corny, upbeat, fun and easy-to-dance-to tunes of boy bands and cute, sexy, sweet, mini-skirted, high-heeled girl groups. With its roots in 1960s pop/rock music (like The Beatles), Asian Pop uses electronic synthpop, combined with elements of traditional Asian music, for a very original sound.

Throughout Asia, rock music was a mostly underground music genre, but – as always with rock and roll – it finally made its way into the mainstream. At first, it was just a bunch of "cover bands" playing their version of American rock and roll songs. Eventually, though, Asians made it their own, fusing it with electronic synthesized instruments and voices.

With its rise in popularity, Asian pop music became a marketing and promotion phenomenon. Now, Asian teenagers and young adults are obsessed with the never-ending cycle of the newest and latest music groups who pump out the lighthearted love songs and catchy dance numbers.

Although paying for songs downloaded from their favorite Asian pop musicians is unheard of, buying pricey tickets to their frequent concerts is practically a youth rite of passage. With pop groups eager for the lucrative endorsements of soft drinks, laundry soap and food chains, you can bet there will be no shortage of opportunity for fans to lose their minds over the next album.

Still don't understand the Asian fame fever? Take a look at PSY, the Korean rapper, and his song Gangnam Style. The Western world has no idea what he is singing. But fans don't care if they can't understand the lyrics when the tune is as catchy. The music video is also ridiculous; so ridiculous in fact that it has over 600 million views on Youtube! Even if you're not Korean, I dare you to not dance or at least tap your feet to that song.

HOW TO BECOME A DIE-HARD ASIAN POP MUSIC FAN

1. Make sure you know all the words to several Asian pop songs, and be ready to belt it out at the nearest karaoke bar.

2. Dress and style your hair like your favorite Asian pop stars. This means trying to look as effeminate as humanly possible. Don't worry about gender; Asian pop music culture is really open about that.

3. Buy tickets to every live concert your favorite groups perform. Be sure to throw your underwear on stage! You too girls!

4. No matter what, as a typical modern day Asian, you are expected to like Asian pop music, even if you don't understand the language.

BADMINTON

For most Asians, dreams of being a world-famous athlete are beyond their reach. Football? Too skinny. Basketball? Too short. Hockey? Too polite. How about Badminton?

For decades, Badminton was considered a cutesy little backyard game for kids and old people, moving at roughly the speed of a turtle on sleeping pills. Finally, though, in 1995, California hosted the first Hong Ta Shan Cup, a men's invitational event. Suddenly, Asians galore were signing up and whooping the butts of their taller, supposedly more "athletically gifted" American counterparts. In fact, in June 2005, Fu Haifeng of China (yep, Asian) set a record of a 206 mph "smash" (a steep downward hit into the opponent's midcourt). Impressive? Definitely.

Why do Asians love Badminton so much, and why are they so good at it? First of all, this sport is much easier for those who are slender, short and fast. In fact, badminton is more like a professional fly-swatting club, so Asians are sure to have a superior advantage.

Now that it's an Olympic sport, it has been validated as a respectable, straight-shot, meteoric rise to the top of fame and fortune. Ah, yes, the most important Asian cultural component: the ability to brag. Not to mention the fact that it satisfies the traditional Asian need to always be first.

HOW TO PLAY BADMINTON LIKE AN ASIAN OLYMPIAN

1. Join the badminton team at your local club, school or college. Notice that many, if not all, members are Asian.

2. Your small, slender Asian body was made for this very sport. Use your Asian reflexes to hit the shuttlecock over the net.

3. Anytime you "smash" an opponent, be sure to bark out loud, ear-piercing shouts, like Bruce Lee.

4. Use your natural talents and qualify for the Olympic games. Get disqualified for unsportsmanship by losing on purpose to get an easier draw. Well, I suppose you did it to win a gold medal...

BEING A PRO GAMER

The modern phenomenon of video gaming is a global sensation enjoyed by children, teens and, even adults everywhere. Historically, gamers used to be forced to stand at a big, clunky machine in a crowded video arcade. Luckily, with the move to home gaming systems and sophisticated Asian-made computers, video game players can stay in their comfortable Gamer's Paradise: their own living room or bedroom.

Although anyone can participate, it takes true Asian genius and skill to become a professional gamer. In fact, whenever big money contests are held to determine who the best Gamer in any particular genre is, you'll always find one common denominator battling their way to the finals in every contest. You guessed it - the Asian Kid!

Knocking out opponents with vicious determination, intense focus and frightening ease, these competitors prove that Asians are truly skilled at performing complex moves, like executing a headshot on two opponents with one bullet.

There are hundreds of popular games out there, in all types of genres, like role-playing, science fiction, space, and military warfare. Whether it's Counter Strike: Source, Warcraft, Starcraft, Final Fantasy or any of the other hottest games in this lightning-fast market, no matter how many non-Asian kids are working their fingers to the bone, you're guaranteed to go up against some hardcore Asian Gamers.

Unless, of course, it's a driving game we're talking about. In which case...well...let's just not go there.

HOW TO BECOME THE NEXT PROFESSIONAL ASIAN GAMING SENSATION

1. Avoid all physical exercise of any kind, besides clicking and moving controllers with your hands.

2. Rely on an endless supply of your favorite caffeinated soft drink for 100% of your nutritional requirements for hours at a stretch.

3. Play for 40 hours straight. Asians don't get tired. Except you might want to get that limp leg of ours checked.

4. Want to become an instant pro at first person shooters in no time?

   - Position your character looking through a doorway, while hiding behind cover. This is called "camping", a tactic often employed by professional gamers.

- Heard a sound outside the doorway through your headset? Don't follow it. Keep camping that doorway.
- When another character walks through the doorway, spray and pray.
- Remember to "teabag" your opponents.Wait for your headset to be filled with shouts of praise from them.

BUBBLE TEA

In America, they have their Starbucks coffee shops. In Asia, we have our Bubble Tea shops. Although coffee shops have gotten a lot of attention over the years, Bubble Tea is taking over.

The signature street drink of Taiwan, it is called "pearl milk tea". Originating in either Taichung or Tainan, Taiwan during the 1980s, over the years the drink spread to East Asia, then the U.S. and the world. In Taiwan, there are currently over 50,000 shops, serving up to 180 million cups each year. There are also shops in more than 30 non-Asian countries.

So, what is this "bubble tea"? Originally, it's a tea base mixed with fruit, fruit syrup, and milk. The trademark ingredient in bubble tea isn't the bubbles, but the "pearls"; chewy tapioca starch balls, at the bottom of bubble tea.

Of course, keeping in line with the spirit of a Starbucks-type franchise, bubble tea comes in roughly a bazillion flavors, versions, types and combinations.

The milk teas usually have powdered or non-dairy creamers in them (because most of us Asians are lactose intolerant), but some shops use fresh milk. Several bubble tea combinations can be made into ice-blended versions (like slushies) in fruit flavors. However, these cold drinks can make the pearls hard, not chewy.

HOW TO BE A BUBBLE TEA DRINKING ASIAN

1. Complain to your server about the price, quality, and appearance of your drink. You want proper bubble tea made from fruit, not that powder stuff!

2. Sip their bubble teas in shopping mall parking lots with your closest Asian friends.

3. Use your straw to shoot your pearls at oncoming traffic. If you get in trouble, do not blame me.

4. Nothing says your a hardcore Asian more than chugging down your bubble tea in one gulp, pearls and all. Try not to choke.

BRUCE LEE

Bruce Lee was actually born Lee Jun-fan on November 27th, 1940. Lee was a Chinese American who became a Hong Kong actor, martial arts instructor, film director and producer. He is one of the 21st century's top martial artists and was a huge pop culture icon who changed the way Asians were viewed by the rest of the world. He was also the only person to fight Chuck Norris and live to tell the tale.

Founder of Jeet Kune Do, Lee was also a philosopher and teacher. He opened the doors for all Asians, and gave Western culture a better perspective on Asian culture and philosophy, through his movies. When most non-Asian people think of Bruce Lee, they recall a blur of punches, kicks, ripped abs and poorly-dubbed sound on Hollywood films from the 1970's. Typically unaware of how awesome Bruce Lee really was, they only remember him as "that karate guy in the movies my dad used to watch".

Thankfully, he redefined the image of Asian actors in Hollywood television and film. Asian males used to be seen as the quiet, simple, agreeable characters. When Lee entered into the acting world, Asian guys were suddenly action heroes!

Of course, Lee only became legendary by eating the right foods, making good use of his free time, and dedicating his entire life to physical training. He happily signed up to be punched, kicked, smacked, thrown, smashed, and constantly challenged. Thanks to his hard work, male Asian martial artists can now be successful actors, like Jackie Chan and Jet Li.

Even though Bruce Lee is the coolest Asian guy of all time, if you find you're not measuring up to those astronomical standards, there is hope...

HOW TO BECOME THE NEXT BRUCE LEE

1. If you're 18 or younger, start your martial arts training regime right now. Anything you did before today was a waste of your time, energy and ancestry.

2. Do at least a million sit ups, crunches, push-ups, and pull-ups every day. Make sure you watch Bruce Lee films while you exercise, for inspiration.

3. Take off your shirt when you fight to show off your super defined muscles. Watch as your opponents cower in fear.

4. If this doesn't deter your enemies, make animal sounds as you fight to intimidate your opponents. "Waaaaaaaaaaah!"

5. Get wounded, taste your own blood, and un-leash a barrage of fury on your opponents.

CHEAPNESS

As we all know, you can only stretch a dollar so far before you lose it...literally. But Asians can stretch a dollar into thousands of grains of rice, sturdy (a.k.a. ugly) sandals, and Black Market driving lessons. And chances are we'll still have some change left over for a nice eggroll or some sushi at our parents' restaurant downtown.

If you've ever been to a flea market with an Asian, you've had the eye-opening experience of witnessing our spending habits first hand. Most Asians are used to bargaining for items as we would back in our native country. In Asian businesses, the main goal is to squeeze as much as possible out of the worker for the benefit of the owner. So we learn from an early age to hold on to our money with as tight a fist as possible, and to take our time spending it when only absolutely necessary. So, when doing business with Asians expect to wait a while – just smile and nod, check your phone for new texts, and hope it will be over soon.

To add to the list, Asians believe family and traditions should be valued above all else. So don't be surprised if your prospective oriental business partner isn't willing to sell out the family's ancient business for a quick profit, like our money-grubbing Western counterparts.

Although we're miserly, there is one investment no penny-pinching Asian can resist: our child's education. Asians believe a good education will mean a better job and life, which would bring plenty of money and bragging rights to the family name. So Ming might not get the newest high-tech item with a mini-fortune price tag, but she will have a great education and a successful future to look forward to.

Too bad Ming doesn't see it that way.

HOW TO BE A STINGY ASIAN

1. Take all the extra stuff out of your hotel rooms. It's free and it adds up.

2. Eat all the free samples you can, while you're at the grocery store. I mean, they are free.

3. Walk down the street proudly, wearing your fake designer-branded handbag.

4. Shop in bulk and use tons of coupons for everything. When you find great bargains, tell all your friends so they can wipe the stores out!

5. Take your girlfriend out on a romantic date to McDonald's. Buy her a soft serve cone, and she'll think you're "the one".

CHOPSTICKS

Perhaps the most universally recognized object of any Asian culture – and definitely the most popular utensil in the Asian cuisine arsenal – is chopsticks. Some chopsticks are the cheap balsa-wood kind you practically have to beg for from your local noodle shop, while others are expertly hand-crafted artistic masterpieces.

As you probably expected, chopsticks originated in China. The date they first showed up isn't set in stone, but they seem to have popped up during the Shang Dynasty. From historical documents, experts determined chopsticks didn't start out as eating utensils, but as cooking tools for stirring, turning and mixing foods. Eventually, though, they made their way into the eager hands of many hungry Asians and unsuspecting, clueless white people.

Comprised of two balanced sticks, each approximately ten inches long, using both with one hand allows the user to quickly transfer (or "shovel") food from dish to mouth. They can be as simple as wood, or as complex as metal, jade, or ivory. The ability to effectively manipulate chopsticks will unquestionably mark you as someone of the Asian race. But, as an Asian, I often ask myself: Why do we use such complicated eating utensils for something as small as a grain of rice?

A word of warning, if you're attempting to learn how to use chopsticks, you might want to have a snack nearby, or a spoon. If not, you'll probably starve to death in the process.

HOW TO USE CHOPSTICKS LIKE A PROPER ASIAN

1. If you're a true Asian, you would already be able to use chopsticks by the time you left your mother's womb. No? You disappoint family!

2. Carry a pair of chopsticks wherever you go. Most likely, all the Asian restaurants will claim they ran out (being cheap and trying to save a buck).

3. Chow down as quickly as you can, whether you want to or not. Laugh hysterically when your non-Asian friends stare in goggle-eyed wonder at your magical eating skills.

4. The final test to being a master of chopsticks is the ability to pick up grains of sand. Congratulations, you now know how to use chopsticks like a pro Asian!

COMPARING PEOPLE

"Why don't you make straight A's like your cousin does?"

Asian children have heard this exact phrase, or something similar to it, at least once a day since birth. Being born to Asian parents, you can expect to be compared to your siblings, all of your cousins, and their friends' children on a frequent basis.

At a large gathering, it's not uncommon to find a group of older women having a "my child is more successful than your child" contest with each other. Any time you get some Asian parents together they'll always argue over whose child is the smartest, or the best at playing an instrument, and the most likely to cure cancer.

Adult comparisons usually include who has the best job, the cheapest car, or the superior large appliance (for the least amount).

Because most adult Asians evidently had to build their home brick-by-brick, walked 200 miles for water, and struggled just to find a few grains of rice to survive, they also like to play the "my life was harder than yours" game. Although some of the stories might have a whisper of truth in them, most of the tales are wildly exaggerated, overly melodramatic, and filled with people you never heard of. Be wary if you are always compared to some "mystery relative", who never quite made it from the old country to where you live now. You can bet they're probably fictional.

If you're an Asian and you were clueless enough to marry a non-Asian, you can bet your entire soon-to-be-revoked college fund that your unworthy spouse will be compared to every more-worthy potential mate, and you'll constantly be grilled about why you picked such a loser.

HOW TO BE COMPARED TO YOUR FELLOW ASIANS

1. Your dad will ask "Why aren't you doctor yet? You're cousin is doctor! Talk to me only when you doctor!" Have no idea what he is on about because you are only 3 years old.

2. If neighbors start condemning you for your less-than-Bill-Gates position at work, blame it on your parents. Claim that you would have made it into Harvard but they could only afford community college.

3. Break down at your therapy session and explain how you are not living up to your parents' expectations and go on and on about your broken dreams of becoming a Hollywood actor but instead, your parents are forcing you to settle for a more stable and professional career just like your relatives', who are surgeons and pharmacists. A job that is a little more "realistic", like a rocket scientist.

DANCE DANCE REVOLUTION

Originally created by the rhythmically challenged Japanese, Dance Dance Revolution gives the player a freestyle dancing experience. This was accomplished by designing an interactive, rhythm-based dance genre video game that prompts you to mimic a strict series of steps to get your groove on.

Distinctly Asian in design, the game was introduced in Japan in the nineties and then formally in North America and Europe a year later. Dance Dance Revolution was an instant smash hit and quickly spread throughout the Pacific, with Asians everywhere manically following the flashing footsteps, and robotically dancing their way to a good time!

The game takes place on a slightly-raised platform with directional, colored arrows, which players tap with their feet as they respond to visual cues from the game.

Players can choose from several different popular music genres, styles and speeds. As you move to different levels, players have more choices and greater control over options. Although you can play solo it's more fun to challenge a live opponent, especially if you want to impress that special someone.

Because of the background images and the rhythms of the songs, Dance Dance Revolution is, essentially, a safe and legal "acid trip" experience. Without requiring the possession or ingestion of illegal substances, DDR is a great alternative to the risky "rave scene".

HOW TO BE AN ASIAN DANCE DANCE REVOLUTION SUPERSTAR

1. Call all your friends over for a Dance Dance Revolution session on a Friday night.

2. Go on the Dance Dance Revolution diet/exercise plan. Survive on nothing but caffeine drinks and dancing. Watch the pounds fly off!

3. Take time out to re-evaluate your life because you are spending your Friday nights playing Dance Dance Revolution.

4. Once you have figured out you have been wasting your life, hit the nightclubs and impress members of the opposite sex by displaying your superior DDR dance moves.

5. Play Dance Dance Revolution way too much, and start seeing arrows everywhere you walk. Be sure to follow the arrows, even if they lead you into oncoming traffic!

DEATH NOTE

One of the endless numbers of Asian serialized stories, Death Note began as a Japanese manga in 2003. From there, this suspense manga went viral with popularity.

The main idea behind Death Note is a notebook where the user writes the name of someone they want dead, while picturing their face. The user has the option to choose their enemy's death, or go for the default (and boring) heart attack.

In this manga, the main character – Light Yagami – finds a supernatural notebook, dropped on Earth by Ryuk, a god of death (or shinigami). As Light begins using the notebook in an attempt to rid the world of evil, a detective named "L" is assigned the daunting task of discovering who is behind all these mysterious deaths, and stopping them.

The story takes numerous twists, maintaining suspense and drawing the audience in at every turn of the page.

After its original success as a manga, the notebook became several novels, a television anime, video games, live-action films, soundtracks and the source of widespread fan writing and art.

HOW TO BECOME A RESPECTABLE, DEATH NOTE LOVING ASIAN

1. Read and watch every single thing ever created that relates to Death Note.

2. Deface school property by creating your own notebook. Be sure to include your teachers' names.

3. Legally change your name to Light or "L", depending upon your preference for crime or punishment.

4. L dies due to diabetes. Whoops, why is this here? Probably should have put a spoiler alert in here or something.

5. Take a potato chip...and eat it!

DOTA

Back in 2003, Blizzard Entertainment gave the world Warcraft III: Reign of Chaos, and later on, release Warcraft III: The Frozen Throne. A mod was created that would create a new generation of keyboard warriors and nerds. This mod was Defense of the Ancients, or DoTA. Currently the most popular port of DoTA is Allstars.

DotA for the past nine years has been perfect for every Asian lover of RTS (real-time strategy) games. In this extreme time-waster, players use one of many weird-looking characters called heroes on a team of either the Sentinel or Scourge, as you defend your own Ancient tower while attempting to destroy the oppenent's.

As in role-playing games, players level up their heroes and use gold to buy equipment during the mission. Since its original release, several games inspired by the

Warcraft 3 map have been developed include the very popular League of Legends, Heroes of Newerth, and the upcoming sequel, DoTA 2.

DotA has become a feature at several worldwide tournaments, including Blizzard Entertainment's BlizzCon and the Asian World Cyber Games, as well as the Cyberathlete Amateur and CyberEvolution leagues.

Enter yourself into The World Cyber Games Asian Championship to prove yourself as an Asian Cyberathelete – because you'll never be a real athlete – and win tons of money, bringing honor to your otherwise disappointed parents.

HOW TO BECOME THE ULTIMATE DOTA PLAYER

1. gl hf

2. imma pwn all you n00bs!

3. you stole my kill!

4. omfg lagggggg

5. suk mah di...

6. faggot host

7. godlike bitches!

8. gg bro, gg lol

DRAGON BALL

Perhaps one of the most successful Japanese television series to make it to the western world is Dragon Ball.

Written and illustrated by Akira Toriyama, Dragon Ball was originally as a "manga" series in Japan and heavily influenced by "Journey to the West", a classic Chinese story. The series follows the life of the main character, Goku, from childhood through to adulthood as he completes his martial arts training and protects Earth from evil extra-terrestrial beings.

The series revolves around the idea of seven mystical orbs called the Dragon Balls. Once collected, a dragon named Shenron appears and grants the summoner several wishes.

Seventeen animated feature films and three television specials, as well as an anime sequel titled Dragon

Ball GT, have been produced. Collectible trading card games, action figures, and a large number of video games have also been developed based on the series. More recent entries into the Dragon Ball universe including a remake of the series with updated graphics, named Dragonball Z Kai. A live action film was also produced, but if you're a true Dragonball Z fan, you pretend it doesn't exist.

Since its release, Dragon Ball has become one of the most successful manga and anime series of all time. The anime, particularly Dragon Ball Z, ihas been influential in boosting the popularity of anime in Western society.

HOW TO BE A TRUE ASIAN DRAGONBALL Z FAN

1. Idolize Goku like he is Jesus.

2. Travel to China and attempt to locate the Seven Dragonballs to grant your wishes. Ask Shenron the dragon to grow your hair so it looks like Goku's.

3. Pretend you are Super Saiyan, and upload it to YouTube for everyone to see.

4. Get into a fight? Losing? Yell louder, until your power level is OVER 9000!

5. Watch out! An extra-terrestrial being is trying to take over the Earth. But, if you thought you could stop this global disaster, you can forget it. Your mother Chi Chi wants you to stay home to study Math and Science, so you can become a doctor.

GODZILLA

After World War II, the most notable fear of the Japanese people was, you guessed it: The devastating attack of giant mutant lizards brought on by nuclear fallout! Godzilla first smashed his way onto the Japanese movie screens in 1954, but only after smashing through military boats in the Pacific and wreaking havoc on the shores of Japan.

So how exactly did this freak of nature which is neither "god" nor "zilla" (whatever that is) come to be? Tomoyuki Tanaka created Godzilla as the worst-case-scenario of the radiation caused by the dropping and testing of atomic bombs. Godzilla's original name, Gojira, was created from the two Japanese words gorira ("gorilla") and kujira ("whale") just to give it a nice ring, not to describe the beast (since it's obviously neither a gorilla nor a whale).

Godzilla is said to be a giant crossbred dinosaur, which was asleep for thousands of years until rudely awakened by the light from nuclear bombs, which also mutated it, giving it some of its powers.

Godzilla's copyrighted roar, although it varies in pitch, is the only one of its powers which remains constant in each version of the story. Its roar is far from normal (as normal as a gigantic prehistoric monster's roar can be), but then again it had to be different if it were going to scare the yellow skin off Asian movie-goers.

But his "roar" is not his only attribute. Godzilla had also been featured with some kind of fiery, nuclear, or radioactive breath as well as laser beams shot from its eyes, injury resistance, and the abilities to heal itself, fly, swim, and fight – all out Asian martial-arts style of course! Everyone in Asia fights this way from birth, even our giant monsters.

HOW TO FEAR GODZILLA LIKE AN ASIAN

1. Practice making horrified looks and pointing to the sky in front of your mirror. Once you perfect it, run around your neighborhood screaming and looking behind you!

2. Make your own homemade nuclear bomb and test it on your pet iguana. Don't forget to film the mutating transformation and post it online!

3. Point and yell "GODZIRRA!" before taking off to run at any time. If you're running a 5k race, this will also serve to momentarily distract your competition.

4. Contrary to populat belief, the old Japan was destroyed a long time ago by Godzilla. It's a conspiracy, people. Make sure your government knows!

HAIR STYLES

Famed, celebrated and sought after for centuries for their long, silky, sexy hair, Asian girls everywhere have got it made. But don't worry, not ones to be left behind, Asian guys are definitely keeping up with their female counterparts.

When we take a gander over the Far East way we discover an absolute nation-by-nation obsession with hair that borders on the pathological. Sure, we all want to be hip and look good, but Asians passionately push the edges of that fashion envelope. Maybe it came from the whole manga/anime thing, or the Asian pop music obsession.

Regardless, one thing is for certain: Asians are throwing the brakes of this particular fashion train out the window and riding the express all the way into the hair styling future!

Long and straight, waves and curls, banging bob or feminine updo, the choices really are almost limitless. Chances are, because of your Asian genetics, you'll look good no matter which style you choose. So pick a signature look and don't be afraid to mix it up every once in awhile with some splashy color or a different length.

One sure-fire look that's destined to please is the standard "bowl haircut" made famous by awesome Asians like Bruce Lee and Jackie Chan. This look emphasizes intelligence, confidence and greatness. In fact, studies show it actually doubles the IQ of the individual who wears it, and guarantees the highest grades on math tests with extra credit. Your Asian parents would be so proud. Another awesome 'do is the "bird's nest". This look is like "bed head" hair on meth. When I sported this look, one morning I woke up and found a chicken laying an egg in it. If this happens to you, it means you're doing it right.

HOW TO BE AN ASIAN HAIR GOD OR GODDESS

1. Research the hairstyles of your favorite manga character or movie action star. One of the all-time favorites is spiky hair. Make it so spiky you get arrested for carrying lethal weapons.

2. Never be afraid to dip into the hair dye! Keeping with the spirit of your manga heroes, you should definitely go for bright blonde, brassy orange, deep purple or shiny silver. The crazier the better!

3. After you get the perfect style, make sure you leave to check your hair in the mirror every five minutes, even at a party or family wedding. Looking good should appear effortless no matter how much time you put into it, but this means lots of maintenance!

4. Change your hairstyle at least once a week. Keep it trendy!

HELLO KITTY

Backpacks, jewelry, clothes, laptops, purses, shoes...
Hello Kitty is everywhere! This all-white, anime-looking
cat has clawed her way into nearly every aspect of the
business world you can think of. But how exactly did
her reign of terror begin?

Hello Kitty, a cartoon version of an all-white Japanese
Bobtail with a hair-bow, is the most widely known kitty
in the world. It's also the best seller for her Japanese
"parents" at a company called Sanrio. The founder,
Shintaro Tsuji, started out producing two Asian
necessities: silk and rubber sandals. He quickly realized
his sandals sold better when little flowers were painted
on them, and decided he needed something a little
cuter to "dress them up." This prompted him to reach
out to Yuko Shimizu, who created Hello Kitty.

It's a good thing the change was made, or there would be thousands of bored Asian girls with nothing to worship, and Sanrio may never have had the opportunity to rise to the top of the oriental "food chain" – right above sushi and egg-rolls.

After taking over the minds of thousands of teenaged Asians, Hello Kitty made her way to the United States in 1976 to use her kitty mind-control powers on innocent American children. And, of course, she instantly became a humongous hit.

Back in her home country, Hello Kitty became somewhat of an Asian goddess. Hello Kitty is the epitome of kawaii, a Japanese word meaning "cuteness" or "desirable", which is extremely valued in the Asian culture.

Hello Kitty has held the world in her cute little paw for over four decades and shows little signs of slowing. She is dangerous!

HOW TO BE A HELLO KITTY FANATIC

1. Go to the Hello Kitty hospital for even the tiniest problems. While you're there, make sure you ask for her special brand of Hello Kitty hospital gown.

2. Buy every new Hello Kitty item, as soon as it's put on the shelf. Clothes, shoes, school supplies, toothbrushes, underwear, nothing is too good for that cute little face!

3. If you have any hope to protect yourself and your wallet from the madness, avoid this extremely addictive substance known on the streets as "Hello Kitty."

4. It is a well known fact that Hello Kitty will soon take over the world using her brain controlling powers. Join the Hello Kitty army today!

INSTANT NOODLES

In the United States, ramen (also known as instant noodles) are a type of Asian noodles that quickly cook when added to boiling water. They're also known for being ultra cheap, and come in tons of flavors. Packets include both noodles and a little aluminum sleeve of spices, with dried soy sauce, onion and garlic flavors, powdered meat broth, and green onions.

Although they aren't the most nutritious dinner around, at least the ramen in cups usually have dried vegetables that magically come back to life when you add water and pop it in the microwave.

Lots of people love these sodium-soaked, crackly-wrapped noodles, but Asians probably enjoy ramen as a throwback to their cultures. Approximately 95 billion servings of instant noodles are eaten worldwide every year. In fact, the diet of struggling artists and poor college students is consists of only ramen because of its low price.

Instant noodle flavors ranging from classic beef, chicken, and pork, to more bizarre flavors, such as shrimp and duck, are becoming available every day.

HOW TO EAT INSTANT NOODLES LIKE A REAL ASIAN

1. Chopsticks please. Yes, these are mandatory when it comes to instant noodles.

2. Make as much noise as possible while slurping up your hot, tasty noodles. If anyone within spitting distance can carry on a conversation while you're slurping, then you're doing it wrong!

3. If you're a college student, your diet is 100% instant noodles. You spend the rest of your money on liquor.

4. How to eat instant noodles like a hardcore Asian:

   • Eat noodles
   • Snort flavored powder
   • Drink boiling water
   • Collect panties

JACKIE CHAN

Jackie Chan is probably the greatest Asian martial artist, stuntman and actor of all time. Although other Asians have come close, Chan is one of the most famous, skilled, funny and prolific.

Born as Chan Kong-sang on April 7, 1954, in Hong Kong, he began life as the son of a very poor family. Although his father was a cook and his mother a housekeeper for French diplomats, they had to scrape together enough cash just to pay the doctor. When Jackie was seven years old, his father enrolled him in the China Drama Academy, where Jackie acted in his first movie at the age of eight. During his ten years at the academy, young Jackie studied martial arts, acrobatics, singing, and acting for over 19 hours a day. Sadly, the academy didn't teach its students how to read or write.

Luckily, after school ended, Jackie worked as a stuntman and extra in Hong Kong films. He finally made it big in the U.S. with his role in "Rumble in the Bronx" in 1995. Now, Chan is a successful and famous actor, director, producer, stuntman, singer and martial arts expert. His martial arts expertise is in Shaolin Kung-fu and Tae Kwon Do; he also earned his blackbelt in Hapkido.

One of his greatest accomplishments is doing all of his own stunts (and stunts for others who are too wimpy), even though he's broken nearly every bone in his body at least once. He was the first Asian actor and martial artist to bring humor to his roles, exploding onto the movie scene as a karate chopping, bumbling, grinning goofball who seems like he can't even find his way around the city, let alone get the bad guys. But he always ends up coming through with his ultra-Asian "Never say die" attitude, winning smile and hilarious jokes.

HOW TO BE MORE LIKE JACKIE CHAN

1. Become an expert at doing stunts. In other words, jump off your roof or a moving vehicle a bunch of times and take the broken bones or bruises with a smile.

2. Learn a bunch of martial arts stuff. You don't have to be an expert, but at least look convincing.

3. Don't get rid of your thick Asian accent. If you don't have one yet – get one now. Watch any of the "Rush Hour" movies for tips.

4. Cut and style your hair like Jackie does: bowl-shaped, dark black and poofy.

5. Learn to fight off a small army of ninjas with only a shoe and a broomstick.

KARAOKE

Karaoke! Just the word, alone, conjures up images of drunken people trying to "follow the bouncing ball" for the lyrics they're supposed to sing in tone-deaf, super-decibel levels. Karaoke is awesome because it's kind of a "backwards talent contest", where the aim is to sing other people's songs as badly as possible. Actually, the only losers in karaoke are the people who try the hardest.

In Japanese, karaoke literally means "empty orchestra", because it's interactive entertainment, with amateur singers singing along to recorded music (minus vocals) via a microphone. Lyrics are displayed on a video screen, with changing colors/images to guide the singer's progress. Karaoke started in Japan, spreading to East/Southeast Asia in the 1980s.

As more music became available, karaoke rose to a form of lounge and nightclub entertainment. As karaoke has grown in popularity, it has given rise to rooms, bars, restaurants and clubs where participants sign up for their chance to sing in the limelight (usually quite badly). Many bars and clubs have karaoke seven days a week, with added dance floors and lighting effects.

Well, let's be serious...alcohol has a lot to do with the affection we feel for this harmless, happy sing-along party. But it's a party that helps us whittle away those nighttime hours, belting out our favorite tunes as we guzzle our adult beverages!

HOW TO BECOME AN AWESOME ASIAN KARAOKE SINGER

1. Practice singing along to your favorite songs at home, in your car, while jogging, wherever. Ignore any complaints or visits from the police; they're just jealous.

2. Host karaoke parties at your house, inviting fellow karaoke lovers. Crank the volume up!

3. Whenever friends ask for suggestions on how to spend an evening out, always mention karaoke as your first choice. They'll think you're a genius.

4. Use your "singing ability" to audition for American Idol or similar. Sit back as your audition video goes viral and see the record deals roll in.

KARATE

Karate is a form of combat that doesn't require the use of weapons. It's a series of techniques, both offensive and defensive, using different parts of the body to protect and attack.

The different styles of karate originated and developed in the Ryukyu Islands, which is now Okinawa, Japan. Karate is taught for many reasons, such as building physical and mental strength or opening up a greater spiritual path. This knowledge has been passed down through many generations. Even in our modern society, many Japanese or Asian people still practice and teach karate.

The martial arts movies of the 1960s and 1970s served to greatly increase its popularity and the word karate began to be used in a generic way to refer to all striking-based Oriental martial arts.

Suddenly, karate schools began popping up all over the world, catering to those with casual interest as well as those seeking a deeper study of the art.

Because of the non-Asians' new obsession with martial arts movies, and their understandable desire to be more Asian, karate continues to be one of the most popular classes in the western world. Thousands of chubby little kids show up for lessons once or twice a week, flailing their arms and legs wildly, in an attempt to get what genetics already gave us: confidence and skill. Although some of these kids end up using karate for "evil", most of them just give up their lessons in favor of something easier, like, high school football. Silly white people.

HOW TO BECOME A HARD-CHARGING, SUPER-ASIAN KARATE EXPERT

1. When you find a truly Asian dojo, sign up for lessons and re-dedicate your life to karate. This means no more bubble tea or professional gaming (unless you play karate games, then you're okay).

2. Dressed in your brand new gi, run around your neighborhood for hours at a time, while practicing your karate yells, "Hi-yaaaaaaaaah-hhhh!" Especially late at night, when your neighbors are sure to be home.

3. Re-enact battles from Street Fighter and upload them to Youtube. Hadoken!

4. Wear your uniform to school. I did it once. The principal said I wasn't allowed to wear it, so I wore it to his funeral.

KOREAN DRAMAS

What is with the popularity of Korean TV dramas?

If you visit Korea for any amount of time and make the mistake of foolishly flipping on the local network, you'll likely be treated to hours of over-the-top, melodramatic, unbelievably corny Korean Drama programming. There are period dramas filled with second-rate costumes, third-rate acting and nervous looking horses. Or you can treat yourself to one of hundreds of modern romance/comedy shows, where the guys are almost as pretty as the girls.

Let's say you're a true Asian, from a long line of Korean drama addicts, who has to get their daily fix. Lucky for you, one quick online search can send you to a website with links to literally thousands of 20-episode dramas. Most of these dramas lean towards the romance, comedy, office-based show. However, there are also "medical" dramas, action, and mystery/crime shows. As with any awesome Asian concept, there are even strange combinations like fantasy/romance/comedy. Who knew?

For the uninformed, first-time Korean drama viewer, here is a short list of some hilarious clichés that you can look forward to in all these shows: the girl always ends up with the guy she didn't like at first, there's always a sharp-tongued father with a gentle heart, every first kiss is awkward, poor people are happy while rich people have tons of problems, and someone is always brushing their teeth.

HOW TO BE AN OBSESSIVE K-DRAMA FAN

1. Even though you already have cable, get satellite television service just so you can watch the SBS channel to supply your daily drama fix.

2. Research all the upcoming, new dramas before they air, including characters' back stories and lineage. This will be very helpful, as most Korean dramas only run 15-20 episodes long, for a few weeks.

3. Take notes while you watch shows, keeping track of how many clichés end up in the storylines. Like any good Asian, when you're done with your list, graph and chart the results in vibrant color.

4. Dress like your favorite drama characters. For the female leads, this usually means lots of pink, girly stuff. For male leads (or any male characters, for that matter) this almost always means suits, even if they work as a delivery guy.

KUNG FU

Besides Chinese food, Kung Fu is probably the most popular Asian thing of all time on planet Earth. There's no doubt this is the most inexplicable of all the Asian stereotypes, leading to innumerable instances of comedy and near tragedy, with no signs of stopping.

Seriously, as Asians, how many times have we been obnoxiously asked, "So...do you know Kung Fu?"

Kung Fu is one of the oldest martial arts, influencing both Okinawan and Japanese karate styles. Although "Kung Fu" is actually a really broad term used to describe all martial arts of Chinese origin, it has its own history, practice and philosophies. According to Kung Fu philosophy, the martial arts are divided into five animal styles: Dragon, Tiger, Crane, Leopard, and Snake. Each style is related to the others, with slight variations. But Kung Fu also has some pretty cool weapons: the broadsword and butterfly knives.

With all this philosophy, discipline, and training, Kung Fu seems pretty harmless and kind of boring. But, thanks to Bruce Lee, Jackie Chan and Jet-Li, it also looks pretty damn cool. When Kung Fu dudes go running, jumping, punching and kicking all over the screen, it's pretty hard to not get all pumped up.

Thanks to Jet-Li, even Wu-Shu (mixing circus-like acrobatics and martial arts) became popular, too. Now everybody wants to crouch like tigers and hide like dragons. Can dragons even hide?

HOW TO BE AN AWESOME ASIAN KUNG FU EXPERT

1. Begin my watching Kung Fu Hustle to learn the most modern Kung Fu techniques.

2. Practice all the Kung Fu moves you saw. Jump off walls, run head-first into trees, slide down four-story rooftops, and hand-chop thick stacks of concrete blocks. Don't worry about getting hurt – none of the guys in the movies had to run to the hospital.

3. Go to a quiet Chinese village with a temple on a mountain and train with your sifu there.

4. You're walking home one night and you get ambushed by a group of bandits demanding you hand over your bag of rice. Assume one of the many kung fu stances. My favourite is the crane. This lets everyone know shit is about to go down.

5. Show everyone your awesome new kung fu moves. HI-YAH!

LEAVING SHOES OUTSIDE

The front entryway of many Asian homes is constantly cluttered with various pairs of shoes and slippers.

In fact, the shoes are piled up in the front entryway because residents and visitors are required to remove them prior to entering the home. Although it might seem strange to non-Asians, the requirement is both practical and respectful. Practically speaking, it helps to prevent residents of the house and visitors from tracking filth all over the pristine floors of the average Asian household. Respectfully speaking, it's kind of a quiet way to "leave the world outside", problems and all. Plus, it's not your house, so you better follow the rules or risk getting booted out.

In many Asian homes, we still eat traditionally: on the floor, with food on a very low table. If you were told to sit where your cousin's dirty shoes just tromped, you'd probably be more inclined to slip those Nikes off at the door. Of course, going shoeless in the house isn't only about cleanliness. Many Asians believe being barefoot (or at least not wearing confining shoes) helps you feel "grounded."

Practitioners of Tai Chi and other martial arts firmly believe being barefoot allows the practitioner to draw energy up from the earth through the soles of their feet. Have you ever seen anyone trying to do Tai Chi or Karate in high heels or Pumas? Of course not.

HOW TO LIVE THE SHOES-OUTSIDE STEREOTYPE

1. Your friend walks into your room wearing mud covered sneakers. If they complain they're not used to being barefoot in the house, smack them with a pair of slippers, yelling "Asian house!" Shoes must always come off, whether you're Asian or not, so don't embarrass your-self or risk injury by arguing.

2. Wear clean socks, with no holes, or make sure you don't have smelly feet.

3. Invite all your 1000 relatives over to celebrate your straight As. Watch the chaos ensue.

MANGA

Once again, not surprisingly, the Japanese have led the way in the world of Art, with manga.

This stunningly original, distinctive style of ink drawing started in Japan centuries ago and eventually evolved into the form popularly known as manga (comic books or graphic novels to non-Asians). Although it was localized in the beginning, manga subsequently exploded into worldwide popularity. With each passing year, its popularity only seems to grow stronger, especially with the advent of modern multiple-media platforms.

Manga covers many genres of fiction, such as action-adventure, fantasy, historical drama and science fiction. With its diverse range of subject matters this is one Asian art form that shows all the signs of an almost limitless creative future!

Although it began as art, manga has also had a significant cultural impact across many different areas, such as movies, television, fashion, gaming and fiction writing. For example, its massive influence on fashion alone can be seen in the streets of any Asian capitol (Tokyo, Hong Kong, Beijing, Bangkok, etc.) in the hair and clothing styles proudly sported by both men and women. These trendy Asians are considered to be the most fashion-forward people on the planet, walking around dressed like characters from Naruto, Dragonball Z, or Death Note.

Of course, manga continues to evolve and refine its art, as it retains its globally huge base of fanatic fans and passionate proponents of its vibrant style.

HOW TO BE A SUPERIOR ASIAN MANGA FAN

1. Color and style your hair like your favorite character, and don't forget to dress like them, too. The wilder, brighter, flashier and crazier – the better.

2. Obsessively purchase, collect, catalogue and store the paperback versions of all your favorite manga series. Lovingly organize and reorganize them whenever you want to have a little fun.

3. Fantasize about how your own life would look in manga form, for several hours a day. Dream about it, too.

4. Become a mangaka and create your own manga. Sure, it's a path of sweat, blood, tears, malnutrition, and lack of sleep, but once you hit the big time, your creation can be produced into an anime series, trading card games, action figures and so forth. Do it for the money!

MASSAGE PARLORS AND BEAUTY SALONS

Asians are rather well known for their, um, "accommodating" massage parlors. Men who so much as hear the words "Asian massage parlor" will end up walking around with a huge...grin. You've seen these stereotypical establishments in movies before.

At the average massage parlor, tons of lovely Asian ladies all wearing traditional Far Eastern garb are lined up for the picking. You can even choose more than one! (Provided you have the coin, of course.) Just be prepared for an awkward moment if you ask for a happy ending in a parlor where this actually doesn't happen.

Perhaps even more stereotypical is the Asian beauty or nail salon. In the U.S., non-Asian women are constantly running to the nail salon to get "fake nails" smeared, glued and melted onto their fingers. As if this weren't already scary enough, they also go back once a week to get them airbrushed, painted, replaced and filled in. Because of this bizarre yet wildly popular trend, there seems to be a nail salon in every strip mall and shopping center in the western civilized world.

Always willing to provide a "necessary" service, we Asians have happily accommodated our non-Asian neighbors by opening and running nearly every single nail salon. These cozy little shops are sparsely furnished, stink to high heaven of noxious chemical fumes, and echo with the sounds of Asians talking crap (very loudly) about their clueless customers.

HOW TO OPERATE AN ASIAN MASSAGE PARLOR/ BEAUTY SALON

1. Name your parlor Heaven on Earth. You're bound to get some very good business.

2. You can bet you work are going to work there with her sister, cousins, father, and mother, six days a week.

3. If someone asks for a "happy ending", threaten to give them a karate chop to the throat and kick them out.

4. Remember to set your prices as cheap as possible to stay competitive with other Asian massage parlours in the area. In fact, the best massage I ever had was from a nice little Asian parlor in Adelaide. When I asked her how much I owed her, she said "About tree fiddy." Now it was about this time I realized this beautiful woman was an eight story tall crustacean from the Paleozoic era. That goddamned Loch-Ness monster had tricked me again!

MATH AND SCIENCE

Next to karate, fried rice and strict parents, one of the most common Asian stereotypes the around the world is: Asians are better at math and science than any other culture.

For decades, western cultures have yelled and screamed about how important it is to nurture little Bobby's creative side. In the typical American first-grade classroom, out of 30 six-year-olds, if you ask them, "What do you want to be when you grow up?" 28 of them will respond with some pretty hilarious jobs. The top answers will include: famous sports athlete, singer (rapper), actor/actress, ballerina, fireman, policeman, and maybe (just maybe) one will say doctor. Notice how many didn't say scientist, mathematician, engineer, or researcher?

Ask a class full of Asian kids the same question and you'll get: doctor, scientist, engineer, and musical prodigy.

Why is there such a difference in answers? Most of it stems from educational opportunities and the difference in the structure of each culture's educational systems. However...as an Asian, you know the major difference is: expectations. Asian parents, grandparents, aunts, uncles, even cousins, all expect their children and relatives to over-achieve in education and careers. These expectations are supported by a cultural standard of year-round school, all-day classes, constant tutoring and practice, and intense parental involvement (oh, yeah).

Another awesome expectation in Asian cultures is: competition. Why is this so important? Because there are billions of Asians, all of us studying and practicing all the time, trying to get the same ultra-successful results to (yep) meet the expectations of relatives.

With all this expectation, competition, and preparation, who would be dumb enough (aka non-Asian) to aim for a job as a low-paid actress or policeman? These jobs aren't bad, per se, but they are not a source of bragging for parents or grandparents, so Asian kids just know better. Instead, we focus on the "big money" subjects like math and science, which all the high-paying, super-competitive careers have in common.

Boring? Yes. Lucrative? You betcha. Easy choice.

HOW TO BE AN ASIAN MATH AND SCIENCE DYNAMO

1. Wake up before dawn every day, stay up until midnight, and study math and science every second in between.

2. Your parents expect you to know calculus before the age of 6. Fail to do so and you will receive no rice for life.

3. Win the Nobel Prize for finding a cure for cancer at 12 years of age. Your father will now accept you as his offspring and talk to you for the first time since you were born.

4. Divide by zero. Watch as the space time continuum rips and the entire universe is destroyed. Nice work, asshole.

MMORPGS

A virtual treadmill that makes you fat.

Mindless Meaningless Overrated Repetitive Pointless Game.

Many Men Online Role Playing Girls.

Whatever your definition of MMORPG may be, it is an acronym for Massive Multiplayer Online Role Playing Game, a genre of role-playing games where a large number of ~~nerds~~ players play together in a virtual world connected via an online network.

Key features that separate these from other games are:

- Monthly payments/micropayments
- The ability to talk to, trade with, fight and team up with other players using a created 'avatar', a virtual representa-

tion of a player created with a unique look they can change
- Constantly changing gameplay and environments (expansions, patches etc)
- Non-linear gameplay
- The goal of each MMORPG is to defeat various monsters and villains with the help of many groups of players online.

These games include World of Warcraft, Star Wars: The Old Republic, MapleStory, FlyFF, Runescape, Lineage II, among many other games.

The genre attracts thousands of new players and is now an international industry generating billions of dollars in revenue each and every year.

A good portion of your time is in front of a computer screen, perform repetitive tasks to gain levels (also known as grinding), fight alongside fellow players in groups, and defeat boss creatures. Its just like work, but the only difference is you pay a monthly fee instead of being paid.

HOW TO SPEND YOU LIFE PLAYING MMORPGS

1. Spend your weekly paycheck in "game cash" to get more gear, weapons and other stuff because you lack any sense of achievement in real life.

2. Cut off all contact with the outside world to pursue your new hobby. The only form of intimate contact you need is your virtual girl-friend from the other side of the world. Well, at least you think they are a girl, anyway...

3. Become an Asian "gold farmer". Gold farm-ers play MMOs for a living, farming mobs for in game currency that can be traded for real world money. Chinese gold farmers make up a large portion of the popular MMORPG, World of Warcraft.

4. Play for 40 hours straight. Lose your left leg for being inactive for so long.

MULTIGENERATIONAL HOUSEHOLD

As a general rule, Asians are well known for taking care of their parents and elders at home, rather than simply putting them into nursing homes. Asian children see it as their duty. Our parents took care of us when we were growing up, and now that our parents are old, it's time to return the favor.

Because of this dedication to repaying a moral debt, multigenerational Asian households are very common, with parents (and even grandparents) living in the same home. This can either be really good or really, really bad.

There are times when this kind of living arrangement can be a blessing. You have the combined wisdom of several elders under your roof to lean on for support. They have likely been through it all, or know someone who has been through it, so advice comes with personal experience stories. Some other bonuses can be sharing household chores. If your mother loves to cook, you could come home from school or work to a delicious meal already waiting for you. If grandmother is great at sewing, you'll probably never need to pay for alterations again.

However, this type of home situation can sometimes be frustrating. Asking for advice can lead to a "too many cooks in the kitchen" problem, where the advice you're being given by one person contradicts another.

Another down side to all this "sage advice" is the potential for some meddling in your personal life. Mom and dad, grandma and grandpa, they all see it as their place to give you their take on your dating life or marital issues. Although they think it's helpful, there's probably nothing worse than grandmother giving you advice on how to stay hot and heavy with your spouse, or dad telling you which condoms you should bring on your next dinner date.

HOW TO DEAL WITH THE MULTIGENERATIONAL NIGHTMARE LIKE A GOOD ASIAN

1. When your 500-year-old grandfather attempts to teach you a moral story beginning with, "Back when I was young..." cut him off immediately with, "When you were young, the world was flat, so let's move on."

2. Never let an elder with bad eyesight and arthritis trim a bonsai tree as old as they are. Better yet, as a house rule, don't let anyone over 80 hold trimming shears.

3. If your mother or grandmother attempts to give you sex advice, ask her, "Do you even remember what it's like?"

4. Any arguments should be solved with "rock, paper, scissors". Most likely, the elders of the house won't even remember what the choices are, so you're guaranteed to win.

NARUTO

Naruto tells the story of Naruto Uzumaki, a young ninja who yearns for recognition in everything he does and aims to become the Hokage, the best and strongest in the village.

This Japanese manga series has gained widespread popularity in the Asian market, following its ability to relate and tap into the interests of young adolescents. The immense popularity of this Japanese comic book has led to the development of a television adaptation. This helps viewers relate to the characters of the story, battling their own inner demons and seeking approval for their actions, so they can feel accepted in society.

Naruto is a manga and anime series set in a fantasy version of Japan. The story revolves around a young boy named Naruto Uzumaki as he trains and becomes a ninja. Though he doesn't know it, the Fourth Hokage used his body to trap a demon that was tormenting the village, when he was born. Because of this, most of the other villagers treat him poorly, as if he were the demon himself.

The concept of the series involves several small villages that are each like an individual clan. This is similar to the way some parts of Japan have really been throughout history. It also includes many Japanese pop culture fantasy elements. Some of these fantasies were originally derived from ancient East Asian legends and beliefs. To modern Asians, it's a mythical story meant to entertain, with obscure bits of truth hidden within.

HOW TO BE BE THE GREATEST ASIAN NARUTO FAN OF ALL TIME

1. Read all 60 volumes of Naruto, along with the guidebooks. Memorize every character's name, history, battles and powers.

2. Watch every TV anime episode of both the original Naruto and Shippuden (over 500 episodes, and counting).

3. Dress like the characters and practice their ninja moves and voices.

4. Go on Naruto fan websites and post birthday messages for the characters, random thoughts about the story, and predictions about how the whole thing will end.

5. Start running around with your arms behind you. I have certainly done this in my youth. Sometimes, I still do as a 21 year old. Asians these days...

NOT BEING ABLE TO DRIVE

Contrary to popular belief, Asians are the real reason air bags were invented. This is why we have flat noses. The top three reasons are: old people, a woman, or Asian. Get all three and you're pretty much screwed. I like to refer to these as "The Three Os of Driving":

- Old
- Oriental
- Ovaries

When you see someone driving 25 miles per hour in the fast lane, you can assume that they are an Asian driver of the female variety.

Sometimes, I have to ask - How did the Asian woman get her car into the kitchen in the first place? Okay that was rude. I'll show myself out...

Anyways, sometimes Asian men are also recognised as bad drivers, but have you seen the movie "Fast and Furious: Tokyo Drift"? We're just like that, because as any respectable Asian knows, there's a pressing need to "always be first in everything". This is admirable in most aspects, but not when it comes to traveling on American freeways and roads.

In Asian countries, the roadways are so congested it is surprising that accidents are kept to a minimum. In fact, most citizens opt out of driving a vehicle, choosing other modes of transportation like bikes (or feet).

Hey, it's not our fault we're bad drivers. God made us with chinky eyes so we can barely see.

HOW TO DRIVE LIKE YOUR ASIAN ANCESTORS WANT YOU TO

1. Attempt driving test. 900 times. According to your Asian parents, this is the only test you're allowed to fail. Never give up!

2. Scoot your seat all the way up to the steering wheel. That's the only way to see better.

3. Take your time when considering which exit to take. In fact, discuss it at great length with whoever is unlucky enough to be your passenger.

4. Ignore any honks, verbal insults, or offensive hand gestures from other drivers. They're just fat and impatient, anyway.

5. Enjoy the results of your elite driving status: numerous traffic tickets, dents and dings in your minivan, and a driver's license with more points than a professional basketball game.

ONE PIECE

One Piece is a popular manga series created in Japan. This story is unique, combining the elements of a superhero story and...a pirate story. Only in a manga would a crew of pirates allow themselves to be captained by a 17-year-old boy named Luffy with weird elastic powers acquired by eating the Gum Gum fruit.

Before he was executed, the legendary Pirate King Gold Roger announced that the treasure One Piece is hidden somewhere in the Grand Line, beginning the Great Pirate Era. Now, many pirates are off looking for this legendary treasure to claim the title Pirate King.

The story is a lot like Lord of the Rings, with the One Piece having many of the same properties as Frodo's ring, allowing the bearer to become the Pirate King, which is Luffy's ultimate dream. He travels with a pirate crew called the Straw Hat Pirates, avoiding villains and making friends along the way.

In addition, the highly-illustrated manga books have been adapted for television viewing. Due to the popularity of the television series and specials, 11 feature animated films have also been created. This has led to video games and trading cards featuring the One Piece manga theme.

The manga and anime are very popular because of the light-hearted humor of the characters and the swashbuckling adventures they encounter in their journey. Just try not to roll your eyes at the Thriller Bark crew of zombies made from shoving cursed shadows into corpses. The series is loved by the Japanese because of its interesting characters, detailed artwork, humor and storylines.

HOW TO BECOME A REAL LIFE, SWASH-BUCKLING, ASIAN PIRATE LIKE LUFFY

1. Wear a ratty straw hat and introduce yourself as the future King of Pirates.

2. Buy a sailboat, invite all of your friends for a cruise, and conveniently forget to tell them that you're off to look for pirate treasure.

3. Soak some fruit in toxic waste before eating it in hopes that it will give you super powers. Also hope that it won't kill you.

4. Become the wanted criminal in the world for hate crimes against the navy. You're not a pirate unless you have a 100 million dollar bounty on your head.

PIRATING

Arrrrrrgh...me hearties! No, not that kind of pirating. So no, this has nothing with the One Piece chapter before.

Pirating – stealing and either redistributing or reselling copyrighted material – is one of the most popular stereotypes about Asians. Currently, the most common type of pirating is internet piracy (illegally downloading software, music, videos and other copyrighted material). A more proper name for pirating is "copyright infringement".

So what makes pirating so Asian? Well, in China all music is pirated; pirated CDs are even sold in regular, legitimate stores. In fact, China contributes the most to the world's piracy problem, with 90% rates of piracy. Maybe this is because Chinese music artists make no money on CDs. Instead, they make their money by doing concerts and getting sponsorships from companies.

Need to update to the latest version of your operating system? Use a torrent service.Viruses attacking your computer? Download antivirus software using filesharing services.Want to watch the latest movies without going to the cinema? Ahoy matey, save that bootleg onto your hard drive!

You would download your own house if you could. Your parents would actually be quite proud of you for saving money. Uncle Torrence is your favorite relative!

Obviously, pirating or counterfeiting things is already pretty darn Asian. But if you want to get ahead of your Asian peers and stand out in the crowd, here are some tips.

HOW TO BE AN ASIAN PIRATE

1. Get out that laptop and go to work down-loading all the free stuff you want. Download ALL the movies!

2. Move to China! More than 90% of the DVDs, CDs and software sold there are pirated, so you'll be able to afford luxuries like food and water!

3. Write a bunch of letters to your local and national politicians, telling them how dumb copyright rules are. Be sure to tell them how much stuff you got for free off the internet. Oh, and include your correct full name and address, so they can come right over and talk to you about the subject any time.

4. Delete your System32 folder, so no one can track you on the Interwebz. Don't do this. Seriously.

POKEMON

Pokemon is a worldwide phenomenon. If you have never seen, played, or even heard of it, you have either been living under a rock, or your Asian parents kept you in a cage for the last decade or so.

Published and owned by Japanese video game company Nintendo, Pokemon was created by Satoshi Tajiri-Oniwa in 1996. Originally released as Game Boy role-playing video games in Japan, the U.S. version launched in September 1998. Pokemon is so popular it has already been made into several anime TV series, 11 manga, a trading card game, toys, books, 14 films, and several soundtracks.

The anime follows Ash Ketchum – a Pokemon Master in training, who has happened to stay 10 years old for the last decade or so – who captures Pikachu first. Ash is with his friends Brock (a Pewter City Gym Leader) and

Misty (a Gym Leader sister from Cerulean City). Later, Ash becomes a mentor to May; Max is with them, but he's not a trainer.

The trading card game, released in North America in 1999, has goals similar to the video games. Because of crazy demand and popularity, this franchise also gave rise to Pokemon "jets", trains, stores, theme parks, and a touring live action show.

HOW TO SHOW YOUR ASIAN DEDICATION TO THE POKEMON WORLD

1. Play Pokemon video games and catch every single Pokemon in existence. "Gotta catch em' all!"

2. Become a walking encyclopedia on Pokemon. You would study to become a Pokemon Professor at college if you could.

3. Dress and act like Ash Ketchum. Don't forget the fingerless gloves and the red-and-white baseball cap.

4. Wear Pikachu pajamas, with Pikachu slippers, while sipping from a Pikachu mug.

5. Pretend that Pokemon actually exist. Defer your life dreams, drop out of college, and become a Pokemon Master!

6. So I herd you liek mudkipz...

PLAYING A MUSICAL INSTRUMENT

In traditionally focused Asian cultures, the only thing more important than education is playing a musical instrument. However, as with everything, Asians have some super-strict rules about what music should be played, on which instruments, and when.

Asian parents think education and musical training should start at the ripe old age of two (by three you better be a pro). Be prepared to continue this training through adulthood, when you can torture your own kids with it!

When it comes to instruments, the rules are clear and the choices are very limited. Asian parents choose an instrument for their children from a very short list, in descending order of "respectability":

- Piano
- Violin
- Flute
- Oboe
- Clarinet
- Cello

Piano is the most respectable instrument because it's very expensive to own, requires right and left brain hemisphere interaction (so Ming has to be smarter) and there are tons of Asians on the list of famous pianists. Violins are okay, because they can easily be carried and held by a four-year-old virtuoso, but they're not nearly as awe-inspiring as pianos. The major instrument "no no's" are any brass, percussion, guitars or anything electric.

As for what music will be played by these pint-sized Asian geniuses, there is no choice whatsoever. Thou shalt play classical music and nothing else – "Don't you bring shame to your family!" – I repeat: Nothing else at all, ever, under penalty of death.

HOW TO BE A ASIAN MUSICAL PRODIGY

1. You're parents will play nothing but classical music around you, starting while you are a sperm in your mother's womb.

2. As soon as you're conceived, sign up for lessons with the nearest musical genius. Expect to make huge monthly payments for at least the next 20 years.

3. Enter Asia's Got Talent as soon as you can and win. Yay, you're not a disappointment anymore.

4. Learn to play dubstep on your instrument, since it is epic. Also, because of reasons. Is that even possible, you ask? Yes, because you're Asian.

5. Tell your parents you're switching to the electric guitar. Watch as they perform seppuku before your very eyes.

RICE

Westerners may like their potatoes, but rice is the staple food of the Asian culture.

Seldom will an Asian person purchase what is referred to as "white people rice" such as Rice-a-Roni or Minute Rice. That's not real rice. Real rice does not come from American grocery stores.

All Asians know real rice comes from a big sack plastered with an unfamiliar language and a few vague English words on it. Filipinos will walk into an Asian store and buy a large sack of rice covered in Thai script they don't even understand. All they need to know is it's real Asian rice.

Rice is so important to Asian culture that any Westerners who are married to Asians forfeit any rights they might have in choosing the side dish for dinner. It will be rice tonight. The next night it will be rice again. Next week it will be rice. Rice will be the side dish for all meals for the rest of their lives.

The only exception to this might be a side of fish, bean sprouts or baby corn.

Rice is quick to prepare and is of high nutritional value. Have you seen many fat Asians? No? You can thank rice for that: filling, and low in fat. It's extremely versatile in that it can be used in a variety of dishes like congee, sushi, risotto, and curry. Believe it or not, it can also be found in fried rice. You don't say.

If you still doubt the importance of rice, ask yourself: What other culture do you know of that actually makes their booze out of rice? Only Asians.

HOW TO BE A RICE LOVING ASIAN

1. Go home stone-cold sober from a house party because they didn't have any beer made from rice.

2. A server asks, "Would you like rice with your entrée?" Glare at them and reply, "That's rac-ist." Order a side of rice, anyway.

3. Leftover rice? No problem. Today's steamed rice is tomorrow's fried rice. This shuld keep your Asian mother from killing you for wast-ing food.

4. If you haven't had rice at all for dinner. your Asian mother will rant like you haven't eaen dinner at all. Proceed to get lectured about how life was difficult in the motherland and how you are extremely fortunate to have food at all.

5. Forget what other foods taste like.

SELF STEREOTYPING

Other races get offended when they're faced with stereotypes; Asians will happily stereotype ourselves.

Many Chinese men have watched a Jackie Chan film and complained – in broken English – that Chan is "typical Chinese" because he speaks imperfect English and makes martial arts movies. Let's not forget the Korean driver complaining about how Asians can't drive, or a Japanese woman claiming that her baby boy will grow up to be good at math. It boggles the mind.

At least no one can accuse Asians of not being able to laugh at themselves. You can't insult an Indian man by calling him cheap; he would freely admit to it himself and half the neighborhood. A Vietnamese girl applying for a job would happily write down "Nail salon, duh!" when filling out the Current Employer part. In Asia, self-racism is common...amongst its own people.

HOW TO BE A SELF RACIST ASIAN

1. Tell the DMV that it's discriminatory not to give you an allowance as an Asian driver for backing into that fire hydrant during your driving test.

2. When trying out for the Chess Club, just put "I'm Asian" under Qualifications.

3. We're not racist. We hate all races equally.

4. Write a book containing racist stereotypes about your own people. Set your people back a couple thousand years.

5. Brag to your family and friends about how successful your book and your discrimination are going!

SPORTS CARS

To Asians, cars are like an expression of our personality. Look good, but do as little as possible.

We like our cars to look fast! That's right, "look". As with anything in the Asian culture, it's more important to have the appearance of awesomeness, than to actually possess it. We don't want to spend a ton of money on engines, paint, or even the "NOS" (nitrous oxide), which makes cars zoom like rockets.

Nicknamed "Rice Rockets", Asian cars have no internal tuning and are slow as hell. Just because the "Fast and Furious" filmed in Tokyo doesn't mean all Asians have a need for speed, or are any good at turning a wrench. Even though the movie showed young Asians zooming all over the city in souped-up cars, the reality is: Asians want to look cool, but we'd rather let someone else do all that crazy driving.

As we age, Asians not only don't want to spend any money on cars, we don't really want to go very fast when we drive. Although teens and young adults actually seem to have somewhere to go (school, music lessons, and school) Asian adults and elders would rather hang out in two places: home and the mahjong table. Usually, these two places are in the same building (not by accident).

HOW TO BE AN OFFICIALLY ASIAN SPORTS CAR FANATIC

1. Buy a sports car from an Asian manufacturer. Toyota and Honda should fit the bill.

2. Rice up your car. Put on a new body kit, exhaust pipes, racing stickers, neon lights and paint it a very bright color (like yellow). Your car should now be able to go 0 to 60 in 2.5 seconds. Well, at least it looks that way.

3. Brag to all your friends about your awesome car. Collect bitches.

4. Park your car in the driveway, because it really doesn't run very well.

5. Hand the car down to grandma and grandpa, because the only speed it's capable of driving is their favorite: about 5 mph.

STARCRAFT

The national sport of South Korea.

Starcraft is a real-time strategy game released by Blizzard Entertainment in the late 1990s, where a 3-way war between the Terrans, the Protoss, and the Zerg is held.

Touted as one of the best real time strategies ever, the impact the game has had on the genre (as well as the gaming industry in general) is undeniable. Starcraft is skill intensive in a way poker never is, requiring insane mental acuity and nerve. Starcraft is one of the best and most important video games of all time. It also happens to be something Asians are really good at, and can be respectably obsessed about.

Developed by Blizzard Entertainment and first released in March 1998, Starcraft is a military science fiction real-time strategy computer game. This game is also ultra popular, having blossomed into several games and expansion packs, action figures, and model kits.

The story line for the game is pretty complex, but that's why Asians love it. Set in space, in the 26th century, the story has three species fighting for dominance in a distant part of the Milky Way. The Terrans are humans exiled from Earth, skilled at adapting to any situation. The Zerg are insectoid aliens in pursuit of genetic perfection. The Protoss are humanoids with advanced technology and psionic abilities.

Starcraft is definitely an Asian obsession. In South Korea, it's so popular that professional gamers are celebrities with TV contracts and sponsorships. One famous player, Lim Yo-Hwan, has a fan club with more than half a million people. Another player, Lee Yun-Yeol, reported earnings of $238,000 in 2012. Major Asian celebs!

HOW TO BE A BETTER ASIAN STARCRAFT FAN

1. Develop your skills until you can perform 300APM in a game. APM, or Action Per Minute, is the average rate you how fast your fingers move. To increase your finger dexterity, tie sandbags around them and practice. Imagine what you could do with your fingers in bed!?

2. Play the game all the time. Ignore work, school, girls/boys, and the need to eat or sleep.

3. Enter a Starcraft championship. How else are you going to prove that your are the best in the world? Also, you need money for all those cans of soda and pizza to keep you at the top of your game.

4. Before you can marry your Asian girlfriend, you must defeat her dad in Starcraft.

STUDYING

Asian students have no social life. White kids aren't allowed to play video games or go out with friends until their homework is done. Asian kids aren't allowed to do anything until they graduate summa cum laude from Harvard. To Asian parents, anything besides studying is a waste of time.

Making straight As in school is expected. In fact, there is no such thing as a good grade in an Asian home. Getting a B is like the end of the world to Asian parents. This is why we are called A-sians, not B-sians or C-sians.

Here is the grading system, according to Asian parents:

- A – Average. This is the only grade you're allowed to get.
- B – Bad. You're an embarrassment to your family. As punishment, you get no

rice for a week.

- C – Crap. Get anything below a C, and your Asian parents will dump you in the ocean.
- D – Dead. Self-explanatory.
- F – F***ed. Get your computer taken away and your Warcraft account terminated. Way to get your priorities right, Asians.

For some Asian kids, straight A's come easy with little work but even then, these child prodigies are expected to study all hours to keep their GPA at 4.0. Forget about going to your best friend's DDR party or hanging out at that new sushi place with your girlfriends. You need to stay home and study. No exceptions, no excuses.

Honor Roll in elementary school, Honors Program in high school, and Dean's List in college. This is your life, in preparation for your future. There is no life outside of academia for you. If you think your life sucks, you will be told, "It builds character."

Fun is a luxurious waste of time that you will never taste. Scared yet?

HOW TO STUDY LIKE A GOOD, RESPECTABLE ASIAN

1. Studying is all you do during your summer break. If you have already learnt all of next year's material, your Asian parents will make you read the dictionary/thesaurus.

2. Score 2400 on your SATs. You're Asian dad will say that is not good enough. No emotion will convey what you're reaction is. That's okay, Asians don't have emotions anyways, just emoticons. ^_^

3. You better get into a good school like Harvard or Oxford. Early graduation is advised.Scholarships are a requirement.

4. Your only allowable career choices are as follows: Doctor, Lawyer, Dentist, Pharmacist, and Engineer. The only exception to this is Starcraft player, but only if you're Korean.

SUSHI

Raw fish slices on rice? Yes, please.

It's mind-blowing how this Asian food ever became popular in a Western world full of picky-eaters who balk at tasting anything not between two slices of bread.

Sushi has become the "chic" food. White entrepreneurs who know nothing of Asian cuisine will open up a sushi bar and know they'll pull in all sorts of business. Unless they hire a white sushi chef, then they're sure to go belly-up. For those not in the know, sushi is traditionally not cooked.

Today, sushi comes in many different forms, enjoyed in countries around the world. Originally created in Southeast Asia, it eventually migrated to China, before its introduction in Japan. No matter what part of the world it comes from, this tasty food always has the same main ingredient: cooked, vinegar rice. Added to this is a variety of fish or other meat, sometimes fermented (for the truly Asian) or cooked.

Other common ingredients include sweet corn, tofu, carrots, cucumbers or avocado. Condiments and dipping sauces vary, as well. Sushi, pressed into rolls, may then be sliced. Edible algae or seaweed sheets are wrapped around the sushi to hold them together.

In the western world and Europe, plates of Sushi sold in restaurants come by on a conveyor belt or carousel. Guests then select the plates as they go by. An attractive presentation is part of the art of making Sushi.

HOW TO APPRECIATE SUSHI, THE ASIAN WAY

1. Become best friends with your sushi chef. Ask for discounts because that's what we Asians do.

2. You know the sushi is fresh if the fish is still flopping around as the sushi chef slices it for your nigiri. Don't worry, it won't feel a thing.

3. Pile on the wasabi! Once your nose is running and your eyes are watering, you finally have enough.

TAI-CHI

Asians are all about feeling the Zen, and Tai Chi is excellent at helping the practitioner achieve "spiritual oneness." This gentle martial art teaches practitioners how to open up their body to Qi (pronounced chi, if you didn't know) flow.

Qi is the energy force that powers every living thing in the universe and if you block your Qi flow with tension and stress, you could damage your health and outlook on life. If you think all of this sounds like some holistic mumbo-jumbo, think about this: Why do Asians age so much more gracefully than the average white person?

The average non-Asian considers lifting a beer can as exercise, while the average Asian will set aside one hour in the morning and one hour in the evening just for practicing Tai Chi, meditation, or some other form of martial art. No wonder we live longer!

When non-Asians think of "working out," they imagine bulging veins and rippling biceps. They think of Arnold Schwarzenegger in his weightlifting prime, or Dwayne Johnson whose arms are as big as small trees. Bulging muscles are great for attracting the ladies but they don't help you attain inner peace.

HOW TO BE A TAI-CHI MASTER

1. Find a nice, public place where you can practice your Tai Chi. Make sure everyone can see you, because that's the Asian way!

2. If someone asks you to do something you don't want to do, tell them you can't because it blocks your Qi. If they give you weird looks again, tell them to Google it.

3. Did you know that if you practice Tai-Chi enough, you can manipulate water like in Avatar: The Last Airbender? Okay, probably not.

TAKING PICTURES

When it comes to taking pictures, Asians always overdo it.

Not only are a majority of cameras and photography equipment made in our countries, we seem to be doing most of the sightseeing and tourism on the globe, and are the least self-conscious of all cultures about how we look while snapping a couple thousand pictures.

Whether it's a family vacation or just a day at the park, as Asians we always have a camera or three slung around our necks, in preparation for the next earth-shattering Nobel Prize winning photo.

Just try to go to a major amusement park, popular city, shopping outlet mall or wonder of the world, without seeing a huge gaggle of Asians speed-walking through the area like a barely-contained mob. Not just one or two cameras for the whole group, but a camera around the neck of nearly every single person in the group.

But the most compelling and hilarious reasons we Asians outpace our competitors in the ultimate picture-taking championship is simple: We don't care how we look while we're doing it. Because we are culturally superior to nearly all others on the globe in education and discipline, Asians are amusingly unconcerned with how others perceive us while they take pictures. We will crouch, bend, turn, squat, and even contort ourselves into unimaginably strange positions for that perfect snapshot.

Want to test this theory? Go to the nearest tourism hotspot and take pictures, then count how many Asians were also taking pictures of you at the same time.

HOW TO BE A BETTER A TYPICAL ASIAN WHEN TAKING PICTURES

1. Get told to open your eyes. Yell, "They already are!"

2. Take pictures of everything. EVERYTHING. Even a wet mop at McDonald's.

3. Take pictures of food and post it on Facebook. Food presentation is an art form.

4. Mix up the vantage points and get different angles. Closeups, bird's eye, out-of-space.

5. Remember to throw in the typical Asian peace sign, akin to the "duckface" of the Western world. You may also like to use the following:

   - Love hearts
   - Horns
   - "Call Me" pose
   - Fighting!
   - Claws
   - And many more!

THE ASIAN SQUAT

If you're standing around waiting for the train, bus, subway, or even a ride from a very slow-driving friend, do you sit on the ground? Or do you comfortably squat down on your haunches for an hour while checking your text messages? If your answer was "squat", then you're officially Asian!

Although squatting has been around for a long time, it seems to be a mostly-Asian thing. Started in India a super long time ago, it finally made its way to Asia.

To do a "proper Asian squat", you squat down with both feet flat on the ground, butt touching ankles, knees spread wide. Even though non-Asians like to crouch (squatting on the balls of your feet), the best Asian squat requires you keep your back straight and lean back into it. Once you master the Asian squat, you can actually stay in this position for an hour or more.

Are Asians somehow "better" at this squatting position? Possibly. Some contributing factors to a more successful squat are: shorter legs, weighing less, being more flexible, and having flatter stomachs. Another factor is being trained from early childhood. In Asian countries, children are expected to squat for long periods of time during formal school assemblies, play time and family functions. No wonder we're so much better at it!

In these so-called modern times, many people are unable to squat as easily as those in the past. Why? Well, surprisingly, the culprit is: modern toilets. In the past, everyone used the "squatting position" while taking a dump, until the second half of the 19th century, when "water closets" (bathrooms) were introduced.

HOW TO SQUAT LIKE A PROPER ASIAN

1. Before attempting an Asian squat, it is not recommended for people with hypertension, arthritis, inner ear infections or extremely large breasts.

2. Squat down with your feet flat on the ground and spread your knees. Eat a bowl of white rice in your hands while doing it for added effect. Pretend you're going to the toilet right then and there. You're doing it right.

3. Do you even lift? If so, incorporate the Asian squat into your routine. It's a great gym work-out that works your hips and quads.

4. Asian squats are a perfect attention grabbing move for alpha males looking to get laid. As an odd conversation starter, you're bound to get people talking to you. Hit the clubs with your newfound ability now and go get laid. Seriously, stop reading this book now if you haven't already.

WHITE GUYS

The average white guy's obsession with Asian girls is not a new concept. How many of you have caught your friends secretly watching and violently whacking off to Sailor Moon? They definitely didn't watch it for the plotlines.

The appeal is the anime girls with long flowing hair, short skirts, and legs that go on and on. There's just some exotic element to Asian girls that a guy simply can't find in other ethnicities. It could be the silky, dark hair framing those almond-shaped eyes. Or it could be the assumption that all Asian girls possess the inherent, err...massage skills mentioned in a prior section.

"Yellow Fever" isn't strictly applicable to just men, however. Surely you've known your share of Asian women who only date white guys. These women are, of course, taking full advantage of the aforementioned obsession that white guys have with Asian girls.

Granted, the stereotypical Asian woman usually only marries a white guy for a green card, but some Asian women have different reasons for marrying a white guy. Like, his money, for instance.

Asian women also do it because they want to be homeowners. She doesn't want to be renting the space above a trinket shop in Chinatown her entire life. And it's easier to get into country clubs if you're married to a white guy. Why waste time trying to make your own life better when you can just marry a white guy who will do it for you?

Just be careful white guys. If an Asian girl breaks your heart, every other Asian girl will remind you of her.

HOW TO TAKE ADVANTAGE OF THE "YELLOW FEVER" PHENOMENON

1. If you see an old, rich, white guy playing high-stakes poker, just sit on his lap and giggle while chattering away in your native language. He'll marry you the next day.

2. While white-man-hunting online, be sure to include "working at my family's massage parlor" all over your profiles. This shows your dedication to family and your expertise!

3. If done correctly, wait and watch as a lynch mob of jealous Asian guys with pitchforks approach your house.

WORLD OF WARCRAFT

As any good Asian knows, computer and video games are the wave of the future. Want to play one of the best of all time? Try World of Warcraft, which holds the Guinness World Record for most popular Massively Multiplayer Online Role-Playing Game (or MMORPG) by subscribers. Is that true Asian super-geek or what?

World of Warcraft, or WoW, was released by Blizzard Entertainment in November 2004. WoW is a multiplayer online computer role-playing game. As of December 2011, there are over 10.2 million subscribers. That's a lot of online gaming geeks.

So, what is WoW all about, anyway? The game consists of players who control a character avatar in a game world, exploring landscape, fighting, and completing quests. There are four locations and several different realms, with players fighting enemies and/or each other, participating in role-playing and combat.

When they first sign up, players have to choose between warring factions: the Alliance or the Horde and choose their character's race and class. Race is how characters look and class is what they are capable of. Through the game, players will level their characters, gain better gear, and defeat monsters through quests and group instances. Leveling professions can also help subscribers to create unique items and earn gold currency in the game.

Truthfully, WoW is the world's most effective method of birth control. Why doesn't the Catholic Church give every teenager a World of Warcraft account? I mean, $15 per month is a small price to pay for their eternal souls.

HOW TO BE AN EXPERT ASIAN WORLD OF WARCRAFT PLAYER

1. Grab a copy of the game (make sure it's pirated!) and register an account.

2. Go shopping and buy plenty of chips and soda to last you a few months. This is all you need to survive.

3. Neglect your job, health and hygiene. Don't worry about your irritating bodily needs - you have raids to complete!

4. Use your Level 85 Blood Elf Paladin to protect your virginity.

YU-GI-OH!

If you think Japanese mangas are taking over the world, you would be right. Yu-Gi-Oh isn't only one of the most popular manga titles of all time, it has become a virtual world of fantasy and money-making enterprises.

The name Yu-Gi-Oh literally means "King of Games". Originally, it was a Japanese manga written by Kazuki Takahashi in 1998, with 38 volumes. Because of the manga's success, it also became a TV anime. The Duel Monsters TV anime was introduced to the western world in 2000, with over 200 episodes. There have also been three anime films, four spinoffs, graphic novels, numerous video games and a trading card game.

The "story" behind Yu-Gi-Oh is simple, with potential for some interesting twists. Yugi Muto is a high school student whose grandfather gives him pieces of an ancient Egyptian artifact, the Millennium Puzzle. When he puts the puzzle together, he is possessed by a 3,000-year-old Pharoah. Together, they try to find the secret of the Pharoah's memories and name, with the Duel Monsters card game part of the plot.

The card game has players using a combination of monsters, spells and traps to defeat the opponent. Launched in Japan, in 1999, it's the top selling trading card game in the world, with over $18 billion worldwide. That's a lot of Yu-Gi-Oh dough!

HOW TO BE AN ASIAN YU-GI-OH FAN

1. Watch all of the TV anime episodes and movies. Make sure you get the original Japanese versions, because only Asians got it right.

2. Bleach your hair blonde and spike it up really high, to look just like the original Yugi.

3. Buy all of the trading cards, walk around with your duel disk and become an ~~expert player~~ immature twat.

4. Use you Blue Eyes White Dragon to protect your virginity. I swear I've used this joke already.

5. If your parents send you to your room, you send them to the Shadow Realm.

6. I would tell you the rest...but you just activated my trap card!

SPECIAL THANKS

To my parents, Thi My Pham and Tan Khiet Huynh, who have loved me, guided me, and sacrificed everything for me to make me who I am today. I love you both more than words can express.

Also a shoutout to William Pham-Huynh; cheers for being the greatest sister ever.

Christina Monti, the butchiest butch to have ever butched. As my best worst friend, you are a constant source of happiness and anguish in my life. When I grow up, I want to be a man, just like you.

Matthew Tripodi, for reminding me I am more wog than I am Asian.

Eav Huy Chan is the long lost son of Jackie Chan, our lord and saviour.

Rachel Edwards, the most lovable squishy I have ever met.

Kevin Peter, the greatest black man in the world, next to Terry Crews.

Cilla and Jovan Nesvanulica, for being a constant source of amusement at Taekwondo. This is because I laugh you, not with you.

A huge thanks to William Bernel, Cindy Evangelista, and Laurel King for your insight and ideas. This book would not be where it is without your contribution.